Sealed with the Spirit

Endued With Power

By Hilde D. Johnston

Table of Contents

Foreword

I want to give thanks mostly to the Almighty God for saving me, teaching me His Word and filling me with His Most Holy Spirit. I thank Him for allowing me to share His truth with others. I give thanks also to all those who have imparted truth into my life. Especially my dear Pastor Dr. Charles Green.

I would like to encourage You to use Your favorite Bible translations along with the Scripture readings in this teaching. Using more than one translation can clarify and make it easier to understand. Scriptures used here are from the King James version of the Bible. The word "Holy Ghost" is used here for the Holy Spirit. There is absolutely no difference in the meaning. The word Ghost is derived from the Germanic. The word Spirit originated in the Latin.

Because of personal convictions I have taken liberty to change certain spellings.

1. INTRODUCTION

T his teaching, "Sealed with the Spirit" is written to the children of God who want more of Him. It is for those who want to reach greater heights in Him and be better equipped to fight the good fight of faith.

I truly believe that it will bring understanding of the Baptism with the Holy Spirit and by scriptural proof leave no doubt that the Holy Spirit with His gifts and the manifestation of His presence is still with us. He was with the early Church and will also be with us to the end, to the day of our Lord Jesus Christ.

2. MINISTRY SCRIPTURE

1 Corinthians 2:4, *"And my speech and my preaching was not with enticing words of men's wisdom, but in demonstration of the Spirit and of power."*

3. THE PERSON OF THE HOLY SPIRIT

T he Holy Spirit, my dearest friend and the main person of this entire teaching, surely deserves a proper introduction. I would like everyone to know that HE is a real person, and most of all, HE is GOD.

HE, our dearest companion and friend is known by many Names. Each one describes a certain aspect of HIS power and Personality. HE is mostly called the HOLY SPIRIT, because HE indeed is so holy. In Hebrews 9:13 HE is the ETERNAL SPIRIT. HE was here before the world began. HE is without a beginning and without an end, indeed eternal.

In Genesis 1:1 we read that in the beginning GOD created the heaven and the earth. The second verse of Genesis tells us that the earth lay in total ruin and was covered in darkness. It then says that the SPIRIT OF GOD moved upon the face of the waters. The word which is used here for "Spirit" is the Hebrew word "ruwach" which means breath or wind. Then in the third verse GOD began to speak and He said, *"Let there be light: and there was light."*

Now let's look at the order in which the FATHER GOD, the SPIRIT and the SPOKEN WORD are mentioned in these first three verses.

1. GOD
2. THE SPIRIT OF GOD
3. THE SPOKEN WORD OF GOD

As I have already said the word used in verse 2 for Spirit is actually the word which is used for "breath" or "wind" in Hebrew.

As I read the first three verses of Genesis chapter 1, I received a picture in my mind. I saw the earth in its chaos and enveloped in darkness. The FATHER GOD looking at the earth so closely that HIS BREATH, the "RUACH", was moving on the waters. Then in verse 3 HE spoke. Everything that was created was spoken into existence by the FATHER.

Just think about for a moment how we, who are made in the image of GOD, are able to speak. Our vocal cords, tongue and lips alone cannot produce the sound of speech without releasing breath. It is the breath that gives life and power to the words we speak.

I believe that it was also true in the beginning in the book of Genesis. GOD the FATHER spoke the words of creation, but the "RUACH", HIS BREATH, HIS SPIRIT, gave life and power to these words.

THE HOLY SPIRIT IS THE SPIRIT OF LIFE. In Revelation 11:11 we read concerning the two witnesses who were murdered, *"And after three days and a half the Spirit of Life from God entered into them; and they stood upon their feet;"*.

In 2 Corinthians 3:6 Paul confirms this truth, *"Who also hath made us able ministers of the New Testament; not of the letter, but of the Spirit: for the letter killeth, but THE SPIRIT GIVETH LIFE.*

Romans 8:2 tells us, *"For the law of the Spirit of Life in Christ Jesus hath made us free from the law of sin and death."*

In John 1:1-4 we read, *"In the beginning was the Word, and the Word was with God, and the Word was God. The same was in the beginning with God. All things were made*

*by Him; and without Him was not anything made that was
made. In Him was life; and the life was the light of men."*

Verse 14 of John 1 tells us, *" And the Word became
flesh, and dwelt among us, (and we beheld His Glory, the
Glory as of the Only Begotten of the Father,) full of grace
and truth."*

In the book of Matthew chapter 1:18-20 we see it mentioned twice that the Child Jesus which was to be born of
the Virgin Mary WAS OF THE HOLY SPIRIT.

Again we see the proof that it is the Breath of God, the
Spirit, which gives life to the Spoken Word.

Some other names of the HOLY SPIRIT are: "Spirit
of Truth", John 14:17; the Spirit of Promise, Ephesians
1:13; the Spirit of Wisdom, Ephesians 1:17; the Spirit of
Grace, Hebrews 10:29; the Spirit of Adoption, Romans
8:15; and the Spirit of Jesus Christ, Philippians 1:19. ·

In 2 Timothy 1:7 we see that HE, the HOLY SPIRIT,
is also the SPIRIT OF POWER, LOVE and a SOUND
MIND.

It is this power that the believers receive when the
Holy Spirit fills them.

The HOLY SPIRIT is not just a mindless force as some
teach; HE is a real person. He is gentle and sensitive.
When people are resisting HIM or striving with HIM
HE can be grieved. Ephesians 4:30 instructs us, *"And
grieve not the HOLY Spirit of GOD, whereby ye are sealed
unto the day of Redemption."* We are told in Genesis 6:3,
"...My SPIRIT shall not always strive with man...".

A mindless force has no emotions and cannot be
grieved.

HE is the one that deals with men and leads them
to repentence. In Matthew 12:31, 32 Jesus warns us:
"Wherefore I say unto you, All manner of sin and blas-

13

phemy shall be forgiven unto men: but the blasphemy against the Holy Ghost will not be forgiven unto men. And whosoever speaketh a word against the Son of Man, it shall be forgiven him: but whosoever speaketh against the Holy Ghost, shall not be forgiven unto men."

I hope that in this chapter I have given some understanding about the Sweet Person of the Holy Spirit.

He, sent by Jesus, came into the Upper Room in Jerusalem as a mighty rushing wind (Luke 24:49). The Breath of the Almighty, coming from the Father through the Son, came to give Life, to empower and to purify. With His fire He burns away the chaff and the things that are not to be in our lives. (Matthew 3:11-12; Luke 3:16-17). This same Spirit Which raised Christ from the dead and by Whom Christ did such great works, now is given to those who believe.

Jesus tells us in John 14:12: *"Verily, verily, I say unto You, he that believeth on me, the works that I do shall he do also; and greater works than these shall he do, because I go unto my Father."* This word is not just given to the early Church, but to ALL WHO BELIEVE.

So accept His Word, believe it, and do not neglect or reject this awesome gift of the Holy Spirit.

4. BAPTIZED WITH THE HOLY SPIRIT

I n the book of Joel 2:28-31 we read, *"And it shall come to pass afterwards, that I will pour out My Spirit upon all flesh; and your sons and your daughters shall prophesy, your old men shall dream dreams, your young men shall see visions:*

And also upon your servants and upon the handmaids in those days will I pour out My Spirit. And I will shew wonders in the heavens and in the earth, blood , and fire, and pillars of smoke. The sun shall be turned into darkness and the moon into blood before the great and the terrible day of the LORD come."

We know that *"the great and terrible day of the LORD"* refers to the end times. Joel then prophesies that before that time GOD will pour out His Spirit upon all flesh. The result of this outpouring of the Holy Spirit are (prophetic) dreams, visions and prophecy.

The last words that Jesus spoke while He was on the earth were pertaining to the outpouring of the Holy Spirit. Acts 1:4-9 describes the event. Jesus had commanded His followers to wait for the promise of the Father about which was written in Joel 2:28-31.

Jesus declared to them that John had baptized them with water, but that they would be baptized with the Holy Spirit shortly. In Acts 1:8 are written the final words of Christ before He is taken up in a cloud. *"But ye shall receive power, after the Holy Ghost is come upon you: and ye shall be witnesses unto Me both in Jerusalem, and in all Judea, and in Samaria, and unto the uttermost part of the earth."* One of the reasons we need the power of the Holy Spirit is definitely for witnessing. Holy boldness which is needed to preach the Gospel is surely supplied by the Holy Spirit. This power we receive from the Holy Spirit is however not limited to witnessing.

Jesus' words were fulfilled shortly after He ascended into heaven. In Acts 2:1-4, it says, *"And when the day of Pentecost had fully come, they were all with one accord in one place. And suddenly there came a sound from heaven as of a rushing mighty wind, and it filled all the house where they were sitting. And there appeared unto them cloven tongues like as of fire and set upon each of them.*

And they were all filled with the Holy Ghost, and began to speak with other tongues, as the Spirit gave them utterance."

Psalm 29 was read in the Old Testament or Old Covenant on the Feast of Pentecost. It is significant that in verse 7 we read that *"The voice of the LORD devideth the flames of fire."* I believe this to be prophetic and pointing to the cloven tongues of fire which appeared to Christ's followers in the Upper Room.

The Apostle Peter recognized what was happening here, and as he stood up to speak declared in Acts 2:15-16, *"For these are not drunken as ye suppose, seeing it is but the third hour of the day. But this is that which was spoken by the prophet Joel..."*. Peter also continued in verse 17-21 of Acts 2 to speak Joel's prophecy and relates it clearly in verse 17 as coming to fulfillment in the last days. *"And it shall come to pass in the last days, saith God, I will pour out My Spirit upon all flesh."*

If the days of Peter already were the last days, then certainly we are now in the last days. We are much closer to the end than were Peter and the rest of the Apostles.

So then, we come to the big question. Is the Holy Spirit, as He manifested Himself to the early Church for today? Are speaking in tongues, prophecy, word of knowledge, gifts of healing, discerning of spirits, working of miracles, words of wisdom, tongues and interpretation of tongues for us today, as they are mentioned in 1 Corinthians 12:4-11? The answer is yes! I believe that by continuing to read the Scriptures given here this fact will be proven.

"Now there are diversities of gifts. And there are differences of administration, but the same Lord. And there are diversities of operations but it is the same Lord which worketh all in all. But the manifestation of the Spirit is given to every man to profit withal.

For to one is given by the Spirit the word of wisdom; to another the word of knowledge by the same Spirit; To another faith by the same Spirit; to another gifts of healing by the same Spirit; To another the working of miracles; to another prophecy; to another discerning of spirits; to another divers kinds of tongues:

But all these worketh that one and the selfsame Spirit, dividing to every man severally as He will."

5. TO WHOM WAS THE HOLY SPIRIT GIVEN?

The answer to this is clear. We must know on whom the Holy Spirit was poured out upon and for what purpose He was given.

In Ephesians 4:8 through 12 we read, *"Wherefore He saith, when He ascended up on high, He led captivity captive, and gave gifts unto men....And He gave some, Apostles; and some Prophets; and some, Evangelists; and some Pastors; and Teachers; For the perfecting of the saints for the work of the ministry, for the edifying of the Body of Christ."*

Is the Body of Christ still in existence today? Of course it is. We, the Church, are the Body of Christ.

We see here that the preceding offices are mentioned together as having been given to the Church. They are all mentioned in the same sentence. Some believe that the Prophet is not for today, but one cannot take out the Prophet without taking away the others. Some say that the Prophet today is the Preacher, but the Apostle, Evangelist, Pastor and Teacher do the same. They all preach. Therefore the Prophet is one who prophesies.

In 1 Corinthians 12:28 we also see that these Holy Spirit gifts have been given to the Church. *"And God hath set some in the Church, first Apostles, secondarily Prophets, thirtly Teachers, after that miracles, then gifts of healings, helps, governments, diversities of tongues."*

If the Holy Spirit would have been given to the Apostles and Disciples only, I am sure that such an important matter would have been clarified by the Scripture. It would have been made clear that the gifts were given to the Apostles and the Disciples only. Clearly it states that THESE GIFTS WERE GIVEN TO THE CHURCH.

Romans 11:29 says, *"For the gifts and callings of God are without repentance."*

Meaning that God will not remove or take away these spiritual gifts. They were given for the edifying of the Body of Christ, the Church. Their purpose is edification, strengthening, encouraging and perfecting of all believers. Also the power of the Holy Spirit is needed for witnessing, as we can see in Acts 1:8.

Why then does there seem to be an absence of the moving of the Holy Spirit and the manifestations of the Gifts of the Spirit over many hundreds of years. The answer is simple. I believe the leaders of the Churches allowed the fire to go out. The Bible clearly tells us that we are not to quench the Spirit. Probably they neglected using their prayer language. Then they stifled the moving of the Holy Spirit by not allowing the flow of the gifts in the assembly. Some might have considered all this an inconvenience or were even embarrassed when visitors came in. By ignoring the things of the Spirit no one then got baptized with the Holy Spirit eventually.

Then suddenly He was gone. Not in presence, but in power and manifestation.

If we open our eyes and look what is happening today in some of the ministries and churches, we can predict that unless they return to their first love the fire will go out again just like it did back then. Don't be a men pleaser or let Yourself be intimidated by the world.

There is a story in Luke 2:40-52. Mary and Joseph had gone to Jerusalem to celebrate the Feast of Passover. When everything was over they went on their way back to their place of residence. They had traveled a whole day before they finally realized that the twelve year old

Jesus was missing. THEY HAD JUST ASSUMED, AND MUST HAVE BEEN SURE ABOUT IT THAT HE WAS STILL WITH THEM.

I Believe that it was so with some of the Church leaders generations ago. They did not keep their treasures, the gifts of the Holy Spirit, close to their hearts to guard them. Then they did not notice when they were gone. So they just assumed that all was well.

Rather than admitting that the fire in their hearts had gone out, they began to teach that the Baptism with the Holy Spirit and the gifts associated with it passed away with the Apostles. The problem with this is, as I have already said, that these gifts had been given to the CHURCH.

I have already heard some say that this speaking in tongues is a new thing and started around 1900 with the Azusa Street Revival. From the time of the early Church until then, there were some very dark times. Some of the truths of the Gospel had been kept from the people. God, however, always had a remnant of those who had been baptized with the Holy Spirit, spoke in tongues and operated in the gifts. The Azusa Street Revival marked the restoration of The Baptism with the Holy Spirit, just as Martin Luther in Germany was used to bring about the restoration of the Gospel Truth, which is, that Salvation is by faith in the grace of God.

6. I AM SAVED. THE HOLY SPIRIT IS IN ME ALREADY!

Absolutely! When a person has accepted Christ as Savior and is born again the Holy Spirit will come inside of the believers at the moment of Salvation. It has been my experience, that often people who have not received the Baptism of the Holy Spirit yet, resent the fact that there is something of God that they do not have. Some might even feel upset and are having a feeling of anger right now in their stomach area just reading this teaching. This truth has been withheld from them, and they are feeling left out. All of their lives they had been taught against it or had never heard of it.

I believe that the Scriptures in this writing and the explanations given must be taken very seriously. What or who can come against the Scriptures? How can one argue a personal testimony and the marvelous fruits resulting from the experience?

1 Corinthians 6:17 says, that he who joins himself to the Lord, God's Spirit and the individual's spirit become one. In Colossians 11:27 we read, *"...which is Christ in you, the hope of glory."* Then 1 Corinthians 15:45 tells us, *"And so it is written, The first man Adam was made a living soul; the last Adam was made a quickening Spirit."* AT THE TIME OF SALVATION THE HOLY SPIRIT COMES INTO THE BELIEVER. In the book of Romans 4:11, we read about the "seal of righteousness" which is through faith to those who are believers. IN THE BAPTISM OF THE HOLY SPIRIT, THE SPIRIT OF GOD IS POURED OUT UPON THE BELIEVER AND FILLS THEM, EMPOWERS THEM,

AND SEALS THEM. (Acts 1:8; Ephesians 1:12-13; John 16:7) I believe that the Holy Spirit Baptism unstops and clears away the debris from the well that is in our innermost being, our heart, our bellies, from which the rivers of living waters will flow. (John 7:38)

Keep in mind that there is a WITHIN and an UPON concerning the Holy Spirit. I will give scriptural proof first and later will give examples of the functioning of the Holy Spirit in my own life.

Paul says in Ephesians 1:12-14, *"That we should be to the praise of His Glory, who first trusted in Christ: In Whom ye also trusted, after that ye heard the Word of Truth, the Gospel of your Salvation; in Whom also after ye believed, ye were sealed with that Holy Spirit of Promise. Which is the earnest of our inheritance, until the redemption of the purchased possession, unto the praise of His Glory."* So Paul is saying, that the Holy Spirit, which was poured out after Christ ascended, is the Spirit of Promise, and the believers are sealed with this Spirit. We see here in the previous scripture that we *"FIRST"* trust in Christ for Salvation, but then *"ALSO"* believe in the Holy Spirit of Promise with Whom we are sealed. This Scripture is significant. It does not say, WHEN they believed, but clearly states that AFTER they believed they were sealed with the promised Holy Spirit.

Here are surely two different things happening. One is Salvation through Christ, when the seal of righteousness is applied through faith. The other is a sealing and empowering by the Holy Spirit. Every born again believer is qualified and entitled to receive this seal of the Holy Spirit, but many never ask God for it. They believe that they received it at the time of their Salvation. We know that a seal is placed by a governing authority, such as a king or other ruling power. It is only placed on an approved of completed letter or document to certify it, or to prove it's authenticity. SO EVERYWHERE THIS DOCUMENT GOES IT CARRIES WITH IT THE POWER AND THE AUTHORITY OF THE ONE WHOSE SEAL OF APPROVAL IS SET UPON IT.

I believe that the recognizable thing about this seal is tongues. Those who have been "Sealed with the Spirit", who have been baptized with the Holy Spirit, all speak in tongues and have a language they can use to directly communicate with God.

Recently this Scripture came to my attention and I began to study some words and compared them to the original Greek. It is John 3:8, *"The wind bloweth where it listeth, and thou HEAREST THE SOUND THEREOF, but canst not tell whence it cometh, and whither it goeth; so is every one that is born of the Spirit."* This Scripture speaks of those that are born of the Spirit. The word, which is translated here as "wind", is the Greek word "pneuma", which means breath or spirit. Since this scripture speaks of those that are born of the Spirit, I believe it speaks of the Holy Spirit. He, the Holy Spirit, blows and goes wherever He pleases, and where He goes, one can hear a sound. The word translated as "sound" in the original Greek is the word "phone" which is used to describe a language or a voice. What is the sound then which accompanies wherever the Holy Spirit is poured out. It is tongues. I believe this is the outward sign, just as the seal put on a decree of the King.

When building boats, installing floors and in other things we make, we have to apply a sealer to protect the finished product from damage and make it imperme-able. I believe that the Holy Spirit in our lives also pro-tects us from the contamination of this world.

Another scriptural proof that the Baptism of the Holy Spirit is a separate experience from that of Salvation is given to us in Acts 8:14-17. *"Now when the Apostles which were at Jerusalem heard that Samaria had received the Word of God, they sent unto them Peter and John: Who, when they were come down, prayed for them, that they might receive the Holy Ghost: (for as yet He was fallen upon none of them: only they were baptized in the name of the Lord Jesus.) Then laid they their hands on them, and they received the Holy Ghost."*

Let's look what happened here. Acts 8:14 says that Peter and John went to Samaria because there were people who had received the Word of God, meaning, they believed in Jesus as their Messiah and were saved. They were even already baptized (verse 16), not with the baptism of John, but into Christ. This means that they had identified themselves with Christ and His death, burial and resurrection. Here we see, however, that the HOLY SPIRIT HAD FALLEN UPON NONE OF THEM, according to Acts 8:16.

Another account is in Acts 19:1-6. Paul was passing through Ephesus and found some disciples there. Though they were disciples of Christ, they were not yet fully instructed about the truth of the Gospel and were only baptized into John's Baptism. Since they were surely believers in Christ, Paul assumed that they had also been baptized into Christ and wanted to make sure that they were baptized with the Holy Spirit also. He then asked them, *"...Have ye received the Holy Ghost since you believed? And they said unto him, We have not so much heard whether there be any Holy Ghost?"* Many people in the modern Churches today would say the same thing. Some have never heard that they need to be baptized with the Holy Spirit so they can receive power as Jesus said.

The Scripture then goes on to say that Paul then baptized them into Christ. After they were baptized, the Word tells us, *"And when Paul laid his hands upon them;*

the Holy Ghost came upon them; and they spake with tongues and prophesied." This story again tells that the Baptism of the Holy Spirit is a separate, true experience from that of Salvation. These people were believers in Christ, but THE HOLY SPIRIT HAD NOT COME UPON THEM YET.

Scripture tells us that we need two or three witnesses to establish a matter. In Deuteronomy 19:15 it says, "*...at the mouth of two witnesses, or at the mouth of three witnesses, shall the matter be established.*" Matthew 18:16 confirms this word in the New Testament. It states, "*...that in the mouth of two or three witnesses every word may be established.*"

I have given you here already three Scriptures to show that the Baptism with the Holy Spirit is a separate experience from that of Salvation. But I will give more.

In John 20:22, after His resurrection, Jesus breathed on His Disciples and said, *"Receive ye the Holy Ghost,"* yet in Acts 1:4-5 we read, *"And being assembled together with them, commanded them that they should not depart from Jerusalem, but wait for the Promise of the Father, which, ye have heard of Me. For John truly baptized with water; but ye shall be baptized with the Holy Ghost not many days hence."*

Again we see here two different situations. In one, Jesus gave the Breath of Life to the Disciples, which I believe was their time of Salvation, the new man coming to life. The first man Adam also received the Breath of Life from his Creator. We see that both the old and the new creation had their beginnings directly with the Breath of God.

Even though the Disciples received the Holy Spirit through the Breath of Christ, He still required of them to go to Jerusalem and wait for the Promise of the Father, the Baptism with the Holy Spirit, so that they would have power, be more effective for God and live victorious lives.

In the Gospel of John14:16-17 Jesus promised that He would send another Helper. Verse 16 says, *"And I will pray the Father, and He shall give You another Comforter that He may abide with You forever; even the Spirit of Truth; Whom the world cannot receive, because it seeth Him not; neither knoweth Him; but ye know Him for He dwelleth with You, and shall be in You."*

The word used in the Greek for "another" is "allos" The word speaks of similarities, but denotes difference in function and purpose. We also see in this Scripture that it speaks of another whom the world cannot receive. Knowing that the world is able to receive or reject Christ, who then is the other one whom the world cannot receive? He is the Holy Spirit, the Spirit of Truth. He only comes to those who have accepted Christ, are washed in the Blood of Jesus and have their sins forgiven.

Ephesians 4:4-5 tells us, *"There is one body, and one Spirit, even as ye are called in one hope of your calling; One Lord, one faith, one baptism,...".*

This Scripture is also at times being used to deny that there is a Holy Spirit Baptism. The context of the above Scripture shows us that Paul is speaking about that we are ONE BODY AND WE ARE BAPTIZED INTO THIS BODY BY ONE BAPTISM. In this baptism, which Paul mentions here we are baptized INTO CHRIST and identify with His death burial and resurrection. Indeed there is only one Baptism which does this and that is Water Baptism.

EPHESIANS 4:4-5 DOES NOT NEGATE THE BAPTISM WITH THE HOLY SPIRIT.

Hebrews 6:2 gives further clarity. It speaks of the DOCTRINE OF BAPTISMS.

This definitely does not include the Baptism of John, since this was done before the death and resurrection of Christ. Anything before the Cross is Old Testament and cannot be considered as a New Covenant Ordinance. Brother Paul said in Ephesians 4:4-5 that we are baptized by ONE BAPTISM INTO THE BODY OF CHRIST. Which is the other Baptism then the writer of Hebrews is speaking about when he speaks of more than one Baptism?

Matthew 3:11 gives the answer through John the Baptist, *"HE SHALL BAPTIZE YOU WITH THE HOLY GHOST AND FIRE:"* We know that this Baptism with the Holy Spirit happened after Christ ascended.

John 3:34 says about Jesus, that He did not just have a portion of the Holy Spirit. He had the Spirit without measure. Jesus was completely filled with the Holy Spirit, but still, Luke 3:21-22 tells us that the heaven was opened and the Holy Spirit came UPON Him. I believe that for those who are baptized with the Holy Spirit heaven will open just the same to pour out countless, priceless blessings.

7. HOW LONG WILL WE NEED THE BAP-TISM OF THE HOLY SPIRIT AND THE GIFTS CONNECTED WITH IT?

To answer this we must take a look for what purpose the Holy Spirit was poured out. In Ephesians 4:8-13 we read that His purpose was to equip the saints that the work of the ministry could be established.

The gifts of the Spirit were given to edify, meaning, building up, encouraging and strengthening the Body of Christ. Also the Apostles, Prophets, Evangelists, Pastors and Teachers are themselves a gift through which the Holy Spirit is able to operate. Each one of them in his own anointing. So, as long as the Church, the Body of Christ is on earth, there will be problems and the gifts of the Holy Spirit will be necessary.

Still, some of God's precious people believe that these things have passed away and are not for today, using mostly 1 Corinthians 13:8-10 as basis for their belief.

"Charity never faileth: but whether there be prophecies, they shall fail; whether there be tongues, they shall cease; whether there be knowledge, it shall vanish away. For we know in part, and we prophesy in part. But when that which is perfect is come, then that which is in part shall be done away."

If we look at this Scripture, it mentions prophecy, tongues and knowledge in the same sentence. If one says that prophecy and tongues have passed away and are not for today, then knowledge should have passed with it also.

The Lord tells us in Scripture that His people perish for lack of knowledge. (Hosea 4:6) So, are we to believe that God would take it away? Those three things are written in the same context, in the same sentence. How can one take out just prophecy and tongues? They are needed to help and empower the believer. Also, where would we be without any knowledge?

In 1 Corinthians 13:11-12 we continue to read, *"When I was a child I spake as a child, I understood as a child, I thought as a child: but when I became a man, I put away childish things. For now we see through a glass, darkly; but then face to face; now I know in part; but then shall I know even as also I am known."*

Paul is clearly speaking in the foregoing Scriptures that we only know things in part. Our knowledge about God NOW is incomplete, not perfect, as if we are looking through a foggy glass. THEN, WHEN WE ARE FACE TO FACE WITH GOD, we will know HIM as HE knows us. When that happens things will be completed and perfect.

At times the Scripture in Hebrews 1:1-2 is used to prove that prophecy is not for now. It says, *"God, Who at sundry times and in divers manners spoke in times past unto the fathers by the Prophets. Hath in these last days spoken unto us by His Son, Whom He hath appointed heir of all things, by Whom also He made the worlds;"*

Indeed God spoke through His Son. The Son however commanded the Disciples to go to Jerusalem and wait for the Promise of the Father. When that Promise came, and the Holy Spirit was poured out upon these believers, Peter related it to Joel's prophecy in Acts 2:17. It speaks about prophecies, visions and prophetic dreams, which would occur in the last days when God was pouring out His Spirit.

Looking around in the world or even in the Church today, can one really say that that which is perfect has already come? Indeed Christ is perfect and to those who believe in Him Salvation is secured. The Church, however, is far from being perfect. Many people of God, in many different areas of their lives, are struggling. The Holy Spirit was not poured out until He, Jesus, ascended back to the Father.

In John16:7-8 Jesus clearly says, *"Nevertheless I tell You the truth; It is expedient for you that I go away: for if I go not away, the Comforter will not come unto you; but if I depart, I will send Him unto you. And when He is come, He will reprove the world of sin, and of righteousness, and of judgment."*

How long will the world have to be reproved of sin? One will have to agree that sin will be a problem in the world until judgement. We desperately need to be baptized with the Holy Spirit, meaning to get completely wet and saturated, totally immersed as the Greek word baptizo implies. We need the COMFORTER of God, of Whom Jesus is speaking about in John 16:7.

All the gifts of the Spirit are needed to fight the war against the enemy. Yes, Christ has won the battle through His Cross and Resurection, but there remains a struggling or wrestling against powers and principalities and rulers of wickedness in high places, or places of power. (Ephesians 6:12) The Holy Spirit of Promise endues us with power from above, so we can be overcomers.

The Bible also tells us that the enemy goes around pretending to be a roaring lion and looks for those who fall for his lie. Only those who believe his lie he may be able to devour or destroy. (1 Peter 5:8)

8. WHEN WILL PERFECTION COME?

I want to clarify that Jesus was and is the only perfect man who ever lived. The Holy Spirit, however, was given to the Church, after HE went back to His Father and our Father. He was given to the Church to empower us to live a godly life and to fight the good fight of faith. The key word Jesus spoke about the Holy Spirit is that we would receive POWER.

Ephesians 1:13-14 says how long this Holy Spirit Baptism, the Holy Spirit of Promise, will be here with us. *"...In Whom also after that ye believed. Ye were sealed with the Holy Spirit of Promise, WHICH IS THE EARNEST OF OUR INHERITANCE, UNTIL THE REDEMPTION OF THE PURHASED POSSESSION unto the praise of His Glory."*

Here we have an answer. *"...until the redemption of the purchased possession."*

So the answer is, when Jesus will come again and claims the ones He has redeemed.

Another Scripture is in Ephesians 4:12-13. It says: *"For the perfecting of the Saints, for the work of the ministry, for the edifying of the Body of Christ. Till we all come IN THE UNITY OF FAITH, AND THE KNOWLEDGE OF THE SON OF GOD, UNTO A PERFECT MAN, UNTO THE MEASURE OF THE STATURE OF THE FULLNESS OF CHRIST."*

This Scripture makes it all clear. The fact that there are so many different denominations and doctrines proves that we are not yet in the unity of faith. The second part of verse 13 mentions that all have to come to the knowledge of Christ, the Son of God. We know for certain that there are still very many who have never heard of Christ and are still lost in darkness and sin. The last part of this verse states, *"unto the measure of the stature of the fulness of Christ."* HOW MANY PEOPLE DO YOU KNOW WHO ARE ALREADY PERFECT AND CAN MEASURE UP TO CHRIST? We are the ones that have to become perfect!

1 Corinthians 13:10, *"But when that which is perfect is come then that which is in part shall be done away."*

We have received the Holy Spirit and the gifts of the Spirit, so we CAN BE CHANGED more and more into the image of Christ from Glory to Glory.

In another Scripture in 1 Corinthians 1:4-8 Paul writes, *"I thank my God always on your behalf, for the grace of God which is given you by Jesus Christ; That in every thing ye were enriched by Him, in all utterance and in all knowledge, Even as the testimony of Christ was confirmed in you; So that ye come behind in no gift; waiting for the coming of our Lord Jesus Christ: Who shall also confirm you unto the end, that ye may be blameless in the day of our Lord Jesus Christ."*

The above Scripture speaks about the gifts received through the Holy Spirit. In verse 7 the word used for *"gift"* is the Greek word "charisma" which is used to describe a spiritual gift. These gifts of the Spirit, or in Greek "charismata" (plural), can also be thought of as a divine endowment and empowering of the Holy Spirit. It states that they, the gifts, are to be with us TO THE DAY OF OUR LORD JESUS. They are with us to give us strength and understanding of spiritual things.

1 Corinthians 15:24-28 that the work of Christ is ongoing on planet earth. Please read the following Scripture carefully. *"Then cometh the end, when He shall have*

delivered the Kingdom to God, even the Father; when He shall have put down all rule and all authority and power.

For He must reign, till He has put all enemies under His feet.

The last enemy that shall be destroyed is death.

For He has put all things under His feet. But when He saith, all things are under Him, is it manifest that He is excepted, which did put all things under Him.

And when all things shall be subdued unto Him, then shall the Son also Himself be subject unto Him, that God may be all in all."

When all these things have been accomplished, then, that which is perfect will have come.Tongues and the gifts of the Spirit will be no longer needed, because God, the Father, will be all in all.

9. CLARIFICATION ABOUT TONGUES

I have prayed with many people to receive the Baptism with the Holy Spirit. When I knew that they have received, I heard them speak with tongues.

This was also the first sign of the outpouring of the Holy Spirit upon the individual in the early Church. Acts 2:4 says, *"And they were all filled with the Holy Ghost, and began to SPEAK WITH OTHER TONGUES, as the Spirit gave them utterance."*

Acts 10:44-46 gives another account. *"While Peter yet spake these words, the Holy Ghost fell on all them which heard the word. And they of the circumcision which believed, were astonished, as many as came with Peter, because that on the Gentiles also was poured out the gift of the Holy Ghost. For they heard them SPEAK WITH TONGUES, and magnify God."*

Again in Acts 19:6 we read, *"And when Paul laid his hands upon them, the Holy Ghost came upon them, and THEY SPAKE WITH TONGUES AND PROPHESIED."*

The three above Scriptures all testify, that the first sign by which they recognized that the believer was baptized with the Holy Spirit was the fact that they began to SPEAK IN TONGUES. Even to this day, this has not changed. When someone is baptized with the Holy Spirit they can be heard speaking in tongues. Some will even prophesy, but they will surely speak in tongues as the Spirit gives them the utterance.

According to the Scriptures which I previously gave, by two or three witnesses the matter or the word is established. (Deuteronomy 19:15 and Matthew 18:16)

It has been my experience that there is a lot of misunderstanding and lack of scriptural knowledge about tongues. This even in the Pentecostal and Charismatic circles.

One has to understand that there is more than one kind of tongue. With one men speak to God, with the other God speaks to men.

Many believe that every time one speaks in tongues that there will be a need for interpretation. I will disprove this by using Scripture.

Some also believe that speaking in tongues is just for a chosen few. I will be able to clarify this also.

In 1 Corinthians 14:2 Paul says, *"For he that speaketh in an unknown tongue speaketh not unto men, but unto God: for no man understandeth him; howbeit in the Spirit he speaketh mysteries."* When we look at this Scripture, we see that the person here speaking in tongues does not speak to men but to God. It says that no man understands him, meaning that this is not English, Hebrew, Greek or German, nor any other human language, but it is a language which only God understands. It is called the PRAYER LANGUAGE in the Charismatic and Pentecostal circles, because with it men speak to God.

Let's look what is being said here in the foregoing Scripture in 1 Corinthians 14:2 about spiritual mysteries.

When we pray in the Spirit, meaning in tongues, the Spirit of God is praying through us.

Also in 1 Corinthians 2:7 it is written, *"But we speak the wisdom of God in a mystery, even the hidden wisdom, which God ordained before the world unto our glory."*

Here Paul said that while praying in tongues we speak the HIDDEN WISDOM OF GOD IN A MYSTERY (Please look again at 1 Corinthians 14:2).

Most who have been baptized with the Holy Spirit and often use their prayer language will be able to testify that at times while speaking in tongues they will suddenly hear the voice of the LORD in their hearts and minds. At times it will be a prophetic word to build them up or to encourage other believers. Other times they may receive a revelation and an answer to questions they themselves may had been asking God for.

In the Book of Jude 20 we are given this word. *"But ye beloved, building up yourselves on your most holy faith, praying in the Holy Ghost."* This goes with the Scripture in 1 Corinthians 14:4 which states, *"He that speaketh in an unknown tongue edifieth himself;..."*

For personal use of tongues, for the individual's direct communication with God, there is no need for inter-pretation. The believers are speaking as it states in 1 Corinthians 14:2 spiritual mysteries.

I believe that while we are praying in the Spirit or speaking in tongues the hidden wisdom of God is being imparted into us, building us up in our most holy faith and strengthening us.

The language received when one is baptized with the Holy Spirit is the prayer language. This prayer language is for everyone. It is the initial sign that the person has been baptized with the Holy Spirit. (Acts 2:4; Acts19:6; Acts 10:44-46)

Jesus says in Mark 16:17, *"And these signs shall follow them that believe; In My Name shall they cast out devils; they shall speak with new tongues;"* JESUS DOES NOT SAY THAT ONLY SOME WILL SPEAK WITH NEW TONGUES. The gift of tongues, the prayer language, is for all those who believe and is needed for prayer, edification and communication with God. Jesus says that these signs would follow the believers. HE DOES NOT SAY THAT THE SIGN WOULD FOLLOW THEM ONLY UP TO A CERTAIN TIME. All that the Scripture in Mark 16:17 declares is needed in our time and the BELIEVER should operate in all of it.

In 1 Corinthians 14:14-15 Paul tells us, *"For if I pray in an unknown tongue, my Spirit prayeth, but my understanding is unfruitful. What is it then? I will pray with the Spirit , and I will pray with the understanding also; I will sing with the Spirit and I will sing with the understanding also."*
Here he is saying that praying or singing in the Spirit leaves the human mind unfruitful because it bypasses the human intellect.
We know that our own thoughts and understandings are limited. Often we don't even know how to pray in a particular situation. So the Spirit of God in us communicates directly with the Father.

Paul clearly differentiated his prayers. One type is WITH THE UNDERSTANDING, meaning his intellect was involved. When, however, he said that he prays in the Spirit, he is speaking about SPEAKING IN TONGUES, which leaves his UNDERSTANDING UNFRUITFUL, meaning HE DOES NOT KNOW WHAT HE IS SAYING. This is the tongue that does not need to be interpreted, since it is only directed to God. The Scripture in 1 Corinthians 14:2, *"For he that speaketh in an unknown tongue, speaketh not unto men, but unto God: for no man understandeth him; howbeit in the Spirit he speaketh mysteries."*

Praying in the Spirit is so important, because we don't always know how to pray, what our need is, and where or when the enemy is planning to attack us. Neither does the enemy understand what we are saying and therefore cannot hinder when God sends the answer.

Romans 8:26-27, *"Likewise the Spirit also helpeth our infirmities; for we know not what we should pray for as we ought; but the Spirit maketh intercession for us with GROANINGS WHICH CANNOT BE UTTERED." For He that searcheth the hearts knoweth what is the mind of the Spirit, because He maketh intercession for the saints according to the will of God."* Therefore when we pray in the Spirit, meaning in tongues, the Spirit of God Himself prays through us according to the will of God for whatever our need is. We see that it helps our infirmities because God knows what we are battling and what infirmities the enemy will try to put upon us. Sometimes this can't be said in a human language.

Praying in the Spirit will strenghten us. In Jude verse 20, Jude exorts the believer, *"But ye, beloved, building up yourself on your most holy faith, praying in the Holy Ghost."* Another scripture is 1 Corinthians 14:4, *"He that speaketh in an unknown tongue edifieth himself; but he that prophesieth edifieth the church."* When we pray in the Spirit our faith increases, as if we were charging a spiritual battery. It is important to remember while reading this teaching that there are two ways of praying and of singing. One is with the understanding, the other is in tongues. Whenever we hear the term "praying in the Spirit", or "singing in the Spirit" it refers to tongues, since the understanding, or intellect, is not involved.

In Psalm 29:6 where it is mentioned that the voice of God divides the flames of fire. The second chapter of Acts verse 3 also tells us here about the cloven, or the DIVIDED TONGUES. I believe that they speak of the ability to PRAY WITH THE UNDERSTANDING AND ALSO WITH THE SPIRIT.

In Ephesians 6:10-19 Paul speaks about the Armor of God, which was given to us to protect us in the battles. In verse 18 he writes, *"Praying always in the Spirit, and watching thereunto with all perseverance and supplication for all saints;"* It is important to remember that when Paul speaks about "praying in the Spirit" he separates it from praying with the understanding. So he is saying that praying in the Spirit is part of your armor and is needed for your protection in warfare.

I had several experiences in my life when it was very obvious that the enemy could not operate in an atmosphere where believers spoke in tongues. Once, when I recognized the workings and manifestations of bad spirits in a situation I bound satan and began to speak in tongues under my breath. The devils became furious. Through the mouth of the afflicted person they screamed at me to stop praying in tongues. The enemy became scared and confused. I also became aware at that time that these spirits could not function as they had wanted because here I was praying in tongues. A power greater than my own was in operation.

Another time an Evangelist came to a little Church in my neighborhood. I went by invitation and even sang a few solos. Soon I discerned things about this man which were not of God. He began to speak evil about another denomination and he did it even during his preaching. I had already confronted him about this after one of his sermons and let him know that he was not operating in love. He did not listen to me and started his degrading and judging comments again as soon as he went to the pulpit the following day. When I heard him speaking again in this manner, I sat quietly in my chair and again, under my breath bound the devil and began to speak in tongues. No one was able to hear me. Then suddenly he stopped and loudly and with anger said, "There are some here who don't want me to speak about these people, so just get up and get out!" I remained and continued to pray in the Spirit, meaning, in tongues. He was not able to continue because I did not leave, neither stopped speaking in tongues. It was then when the real spirit in him manifested. Then suddenly he verbally attacked a few people in the congregation. At that point the Pastor of the Church came walking to the pulpit. Having recognized now what kind of a person he had before him, he said to the man that he was out of order. The Pastors wife at that time also walked up and told him that he was not allowed to continue speaking in that Church.

The "Evangelist" grabbed his Bible and stormed out of the Church.

Because of some of these experiences I appreciate and greatly value these gifts of the Spirit in my life

I know that there are precious people who dearly love God with all their heart, but because of a lack of understanding of these biblical truths, have never laid claim to everything God made available to them. The prayer language is a God given tool for all believers to build themselves up in the Most Holy Ghost, to commune with God and for spiritual warfare. We know that God is not a respecter of persons, meaning that He shows no partiality, according to what Peter said about this matter (Acts 10:34).

TONGUES, THE PRAYER LANGUAGE IS NEEDED BY ALL AND THEREFORE IS AVAILABLE TO ALL WHO ARE BELIEVERS.

The second kind of tongue is not the prayer language, but is something first spoken about in the Book of Isaiah 28:11. It says, *"For with stammering lips and another tongue will He speak to His people."*

We see here that HE, God, is doing the speaking with *"stammering lips and another tongue,..."* We know that God uses people as His mouthpiece. Since God is doing the speaking in this instance, it is a prophetic tongue and therefore needs interpretation.

In 1 Corinthians 14:12-13 *Paul* says, *"Even so ye, for as much as ye are zealous for spiritual gifts; seek that ye may excel to the edifying of the Church."* We see here that it was more important to Paul to see others blessed through the prophetic and that the Church be edified and strengthened rather than just he, himself, by using his prayer language.

There is a great blessing which happens when one speaks in tongues. The person using tongues thereby is edified, strengthened, encouraged and comforted. This speaks about the prayer language.

However, the kind of tongue about which we are speaking now is the prophetic tongue, which is always directed to the Church and therefore needs to be interpreted that it may be understood and be of benefit to the hearer.

Then there is regular prophecy which is spoken in the language of the people to whom it is given. There is power in the spoken word. Blessing and cursing both come out of the mouth. Paul reminds Timothy in 1 Timothy 1:18,

"This charge I commit unto thee, son Timothy, according to the prophecies which went before on thee, that by them thou mightest war a good warfare." He also writes in Romans 1:11, *"For I long to see you, that I may impart unto you some spiritual gift, to the end you may be*

established." **We see here that individual gifts were also imparted by the laying on of hands and the prophetic word. They are literally spoken into the believers lives.**

We see that a word from God through one who prophesies, as well as from the promises of His written Word, will encourage the believer and give renewed hope and comfort. It will be something to stand on and hold on to. Timothy had received a prophetic word. He was to use it and remember it when things got rough.

Paul says in 1 Corinthians 14:4, *" He that speaketh in an unknown tongue edifieth himself; but he that prophesieth edifieth the Church."* In verses 18-19 in the same chapter he writes, *"...I thank my God, I speak with tongues more than you all: Yet in the Church I had rather speak five words with the understanding, that by my voice I might teach others also, than thousand word in an unknown tongue."* In other words, Paul spoke in tongues more than anyone he knew. The important thing is that he differentiated between tongues spoken for his own edification and fellowship with God and the tongues spoken in the Church. In verse 19, *"Yet in the Church..."*, Paul is saying he would rather edify the whole Church by prophecy directly or by interpretation of a tongue, rather than just being edified himself. By no means does he forbid speaking in tongues in the Church for one's personal edification, but he says that he would RATHER edify the whole Church. The importance of the prayer language is surely thereby not devalued. Remember that 1 Corinthians 14:40 tells us, that all things must be done decently and in order.

After having received the Baptism of the Holy Spirit, tongues will be there and can and should be used at will. No special unction is needed to use Your prayer language, even though there will be an unction at times. It

should be used as much as possible to gain strength or to let the Holy Spirit intercede through You.

Remember that 1 Corinthians 14:4, says that speaking in tongues will edify (strengthen) You by the Holy Spirit.

When one gives a prophecy in tongues it must be interpreted, since it is directed to the Church. An unction or leading of the Holy Spirit to do this is necessary. The same is true if the prophecy is given in an understandable language such as English. If God wants the person to give it to the Church, there will be an urgency to speak. In Jeremiah 20:9 the Prophet says, *"Then I said, that I will not make mention of Him, nor speak any more in His Name. But the Word was in mine heart as a fire shut up in my bones and I could not stay."* Jeremiah here was upset at God, because every time that He spoke in the Name of the Lord he was mocked and harassed. Though he did not want to prophesy anymore, he could not contain it and so spoke it out anyway.

1 Corinthians 14:32 tell us, *"The spirits of the Prophets are subject to the Prophets"*, meaning that God will not force someone to prophesy. He will encourage and urge the person to speak, however, the person has to be willing and obedient.

10. TO THE CHURCH LEADERS AND PAS-TORS

I n 1 Corinthians 14:39 we read, *Wherefore, brethren, covet to prophesy, and do not forbid to speak with tongues,"* and in 1 Thessalonians 5:19-20 Paul says, *"Quench not the Spirit. Despise not prophesying."*

We see in these Scriptures that there are some things that are not to be done. That is, as we can see in the foregoing Scriptures, not allowing to speak in tongues is stifling and hindering the Holy Spirit. To quench something means to put it out as one would put out a fire. Three times in the foregoing scriptures are we told not to hinder the Holy Spirits moving in the Churches. This makes it of utmost importance to be obeyed. We must allow the Spirit of God to be in charge in our assemblies and to let Him move as HE desires.

When the Holy Spirit is quenched, His fire cannot purify and cleanse us, His power cannot strengthen and heal us, nor His Word refresh us and revive us.

The Pastor who has the responsibility before God to feed and equip the people God has placed in his care must not withhold anything from them which will help them in their battles. The Baptism in the Holy Spirit is not an option but a necessity. It is so important that Peter and John left from Jerusalem for Samaria as soon as they heard that there were believers in Samaria. Remember that they most likely had to walk wherever they went.

What a blessing it is to walk into a Church where the Holy Spirit is allowed control. Often the presence of the

Spirit can be strongly felt. I have been in gatherings where there was such a strong presence of God that one could feel Him with every breath that was taken and also could see Him on the people. I have felt the Glory of God like a blanket, or weight covering me. The word used in 2 Chronicles 5:14; 7:1; 7:2 and 7:3 for glory, is also used to say "weight," in Hebrew.

Paul speaks also about singing in the Spirit and differentiates it with singing with the understanding. 1 Corinthians 14:5 he says, *"...I will sing in the Spirit, and I will sing with the understanding also."* So the same way we can pray in the Spirit, or give a prophetic word in tongues so we can lift up the Lord with a spiritual song of thanksgiving, praise and worship. Singing in the Spirit should also be given a place in both, personal and congregational worship. However, everything must be done decently and in order, since confusion is not of God.

Ephesians 5:18-19 says, *"And be not drunk with wine, wherein is excess; but be filled with the Spirit, speaking to one another in psalms and hymns and spiritual songs, singing and making melody in your heart to the Lord."*

What a heavenly sound it is when God's people in the assembly lift up a song to the Lord, singing in tongues. Then the instrument players each use their instruments in a free sound which comes from the heart, all separate, each worshipping God in their own way, but yet all in unison.

It is truly a heavenly sound which one has to hear who has never experienced it in order to comprehend it. It sounds as if thousands of angels are singing.

It is during this form of worship, when the greatest manifestations of the gifts of the Holy Spirit occur, such as prophecy, healing, and the word of knowledge.

There is even power in prayer after one is baptized with the Holy Spirit. The difference is notable.

Following programs and rituals, in some Churches, there is no place or time for the Holy Spirit to move. The people are crying out for revival, yet the One Who wants to revive them is not allowed access or control.

In many of these Churches people who have been baptized with the Holy Spirit and speak with tongues will not be allowed to do anything in that Church, no matter how great of a gift or talent they may have. What a tragedy! Many rely and make their boast in the natural abilities or professionalism of their musicians who sing well and play the instruments well, but have no anointing. Without the anointing nothing happens in the Spirit. The Word of God tells us that it is the anointing that breaks the yoke (Isaiah 10:27). This means that bondages are being broken and people are being set free by the anointing of the Holy Spirit.

At times God might send a messenger with a certain word or anointing to a Church or another group of people to test their willingness to receive. If they welcome the messenger, knowing his or her message and anointing, they will also receive the Spirit and what God wants to do in their midst.

John 13:20 says, *"Verily, verily, I say unto you, HE THAT RECEIVETH WHOMSOEVER I SEND RECEIVETH ME; AND HE THAT RECEIVETH ME RECEIVETH HIM THAT SENT ME"* The contrary must be true when God's people are not received.

Sadly enough there are some Pastors and leaders in the Church who really have been touched by the Holy Spirit and who know that the Baptism with the Holy Spirit is for now and the gifts are real. Because they don't want to loose their income from their denominational head quarters they will withhold this truth from their congregations. The knowledge of these truths would so much empower the believers to have greater victories in their lives.

In John 10:11-15 Jesus speaks of the good shepherd. The good shepherd cares for his sheep. He would even lay down his life for them. In contrast to this the hired person does not love the sheep and only takes care of them for money.

A few years ago I was asked by a friend to come to her house and share concerning the Baptism of the Holy Spirit with her daughter and several of her friends who went to a traditional Church, where the Baptism with the Holy Spirit was not taught. After I was done with the teaching, I laid hands on them and they received the Holy Spirit and spoke in tongues.

One of the young women was so excited about what happened to her that she began to share with others in the Church she was attending. I began to receive phone calls from friends of hers, who also wanted to receive it. So they came to my meetings and to my house to get baptized with the Holy Spirit. All received and spoke with tongues.

Then the same young woman invited me to a prayer meeting at the Church were she went. I did not want to go at first, but I prayed about it and then went.

I sat at a large round table with at least six ladies sitting there. During prayer time one of the ladies at the table kept on praying. "Please, Lord, fill me with your Holy Spirit. I want you to fill me" Listening to her, the Holy Spirit spoke to me. "She is crying out for me. Tell her she can have the Holy Spirit now and receive her prayer language."

After the meeting, I told her what the Holy Spirit had said to me. Other people around her must have heard me tell her this. So they all started walking towards me. Then one lady began to weep uncontrollably. As she walked towards me the Holy Spirit already began to touch her. By the time she got to me she was almost on the floor, face flushed, unable to speak and crying uncontrollably. As soon as I touched her she broke out speaking in tongues, tears rolling.

One young lady after another then came and received the Holy Spirit. Including the one God had given me that word for.

Then the Pastor became aware of what was going on and came walking over. Realizing that this was something God was doing, he just silently laid his hand on the crying woman.

I later told him that he himself needed to get baptized with the Holy Spirit, since many people from his congregation were coming to me and going somewhere else to get it. He, however, was not ready to surrender to the Holy Spirit.

I here have shared some personal testimonies only for the purpose of letting the reader know that this, what I am writing about, is real and operating in my life. You can be used as well.

There are countless people in the world today who are witnesses that the gifts Paul wrote about are active today, having experienced these gifts in their own lives. I, myself am one of them, who has been blessed by the gifts of others. I have received unexpected healings and deliverance even while I was watching television and therefore greatly respect the gift in others. I, myself also being an instrument to touch peoples' lives with prophecy, word of wisdom, word of knowledge, discerning of spirits, healing and tongues. I know the life changing power of the gifts of the Holy Spirit. Many witnesses could confirm this statement.

Some readers may think this may be for someone else, but maybe it is not for them.

Often misunderstood is 1 Corinthians 12:30, *"Have all the gifts of healing? Do all speak with tongues? Do all interpret?"* Here Paul speaks about the gifts of the Spirit and is referring to the prophetic tongue. Remember that with the prayer language men speak to God. With the prophetic tongue God speaks to men. It must be interpreted either by the one who gives it, or the one who hears it, since it is to strengthen and build up the Church. It is a prophecy and not everyone has a prophetic gift. Since the prayer language is a weapon of war for the believer, it is for all who have been born again.

2 Corinthians 10:3-4 tells us; *"For though we walk in the flesh, we do not war after the flesh: (For the weapons of our warfare are not carnal, but mighty through God to the pulling down of strongholds;)*

This tells us that we do not fight our wars with natural weapons, but with the power of the Holy Spirit.

In Acts 2 the tongues were human languages. It says that there were in Jerusalem devout men form every nation under the sun. Yet every man was able to understand the upper room group because they all heard them speak in their own language about God's marvelous works. At times a believer who has never learned a particular language will actually speak in a foreign language. The tongues sometimes will be understood by someone, as if it were spoken in their own language.

In 1990 I personally had this experience. I had ministered in a New Orleans nursing home and have prayed with many of the residents there who then received Jesus

Christ as their Lord and Savior. One of the employees asked me to visit with a Vietnamese woman and pray with her because she was very ill.

When I walked into the woman's room I discovered that she did not speak English. I was grieved for a moment, because I thought at first that I would not be able to communicate with her and tell her of God's Salvation. I began to weep, tears running down my face. Then I spoke to the Lord. "It wouldn't be fair that this woman should not hear the Gospel just because I don't speak Vietnamese. I want You to speak to her in her own language, as I speak in tongues."

I then opened my mouth and by faith began to speak in tongues. It sounded like an oriental language. The tongues came out in Vietnamese. The woman looked at me. Her eyes became big and she began to weep. Streams of tears were running down her face. It was obvious that she understood. The employee who had guided me into her room witnessed it and was speechless at first. She then declared to me, "You were speaking in Vietnamese!" As I looked at the Vietnamese woman, her face was lit up. The Glory of the Lord could be seen on her.

I have heard since then of other people who had similar experiences.

In 1 Corinthians 13:1 we see that there are tongues of men and tongues of angels, *"Though I speak with the tongues of men and of angels, and have not charity, I am become as sounding brass, or a tinkling cymbal."*

According to Galations 3:14 we receive the promise of the Spirit by faith. *"That the blessings of Abraham might come on the Gentiles through Jesus Christ; that we might receive the Promise of the Spirit though faith."* We see that even the Baptism of the Holy Spirit, which is the Promise of the Father, and every gift He gives, we receive only through faith. As the Holy Spirit is received by faith, faith works by love. Galatians 5:6 tells us, *"...but faith which worketh by love."*

No matter what. Love makes it all work. Love conquers all.

From this very same nursing home I have many other precious memories. I started going to this home to minister to the residents, and I did. Many residents of this home gave their hearts to the Lord. One of the supervisors recognized that I operated in the word of knowledge and in the prophetic as well, and she began to ask the employees if they wanted prayer. To my surprise a line began to form of about 19-25 employees who all wanted prayer and some were hoping that they would possibly receive a prophetic word. I was led into a room. As soon as I walked into this room, I actually could feel the Holy Spirit blowing in like a warm breeze. Having felt this, I know that God was there and that He would bless those that came that day, including myself. Then one by one they entered. Many indeed were blessed by the word of knowledge and a prophetic word. This happened on more than one occasion in this same nursing home.

On one of the occasions a man in his fifties, wheelchair bound due to a possible neurological problem rolled himself into the room where I was with the employees. He was unable to walk and also had a problem to verbally communicate, but motioned that he wanted prayer. I then prayed for him. The next time I visited this home, he was walking all around and was able to communicate verbally. I have never seen him in a wheelchair again since that day.

I can testify that on many other occasions the Spirit of the Lord was working powerfully through me. Some of the stories I do not feel free to share.

These things happened only because the Spirit of the LORD was working through me at that time. It is something that cannot be done at will and one has to be an open and willing vessel.

11. OTHER GIFTS ASSOCIATED WITH THE BAPTISM OF THE HOLY SPIRIT

There are also other gifts related to the Holy Spirit besides speaking in tongues and prophecy. These are found in 1Corinthians 12:4-11. *"Now there are diversities of gifts, but the same Spirit. And there are diversities of administrations, but the same Lord. And there are diversities of operations, but it is the same God which worketh all in all. But the manifestatin of the Spirit is given to every man to profit withal. For to one is given by the Spirit the word of wisdom; to another the word of knowledge by the same Spirit; to another faith by the same Spirit; to another gifts of healing by the same Spirit; to another working of miracles; to another prophecy; to another discerning of Spirits; to another divers kinds of tongues; to another the interpretation of tongues: But all these worketh that one and the selfsame Spirit, dividing to every man severally as He will."*

There are a total of nine gifts of the Holy Spirit. Remember that these gifts were all given to help the Church, even in our time. There is nothing in the Bible where it says that they have been taken away. They all are much needed. Some believers have more than one of these gifts operating together for the good of the Church and to help the individual believer. Certain individuals operate to a degree in all of them, but there will be some gifts which are the strongest.

In this teaching I will write what I believe to be the most important points about these gifts. There is, however, a lot more to learn about them. Please study them more. They are great treasures in the arsenal of the Church and in the lives of the believers. Don't confuse the gifts of the Holy Spirit with the fruits of the Spirit. The gifts are given, imparted by God. The believer has to grow and develop the fruits of the Spirit in his or her own character as they grow in Christ (Galatians 5:22-25).

Following is an introduction to the gifts:

1) The Word of Wisdom

The believers who have the word of wisdom have a counseling gift. They will use the knowledge of a situation and apply the Word of God to it. In order to give this word of wisdom they also need discernment of the entire situation. They often operate to a degree in the word of knowledge and the gift of discernment of spirits. They give their advice cautiously considering the whole picture. Almost like a chess player, they take into account what next move the enemy might make. Remember that God's Word must be the standard for any advise given and decision made.

2) The Word of Knowledge

The word of knowledge is a supernatural ability to see and discern a situation as it really is. As I am in front of people to pray with them, I will often see or hear inside of me how many children they have, what job they are in, or even what sin is in their lives. The Lord will even tell me at times whether they have a pet or not. The Holy Spirit will reveal only that which needs to be known to help the individual or to protect and warn the one who ministers. The person who operates in this gift is not able to use it at will, only as the Holy Spirit reveals it and allows it. This person is not a psychic, nor a fortune teller who obtains his or her knowledge from other sources.

3) The Gift of Faith

As I have written earlier, faith works by love. We all have been given a measure of faith. (Romans 12:3) If such a small amount of faith, such as the size of a mustard seed can speak to a mountain and cast it into the sea, the people with the gift of faith have been given more than the size of a mustard seed. (Matthew 13:31; Mark 4:31; Luke17:6)

They make great intercessors and will not easily be shaken.

4) Gifts of Healing

It speaks here of gifts (plural) of healing. There are some believers who have great faith to pray for certain diseases and people are being healed. God wants every disease to be gone. Jesus did not just purchase our Salvation with His precious Blood but also paid for our healings with the stripes on His Body. (1 Peter 2:24) It is God's will that we are healthy. 3 John verse 2 says, *"Beloved, I wish above all things that thou mayest prosper, and be in health, even as thy soul prospereth."*

Jesus went around healing all kinds of sicknesses. He cleansed and healed the lepers and raised the dead. There are many accounts in the Gospels.

In Matthew 10:8, Jesus gives the command to His Disciples saying, *"Heal the sick, cleans the lepers, raise the dead, cast out devils; freely ye have received, freely give."*

I often hear people praying, saying "Lord, please heal them if it is Your will." Looking at the foregoing Scriptures, how can one think that it is not His will to have His people well. Remember His statement that He came that we should have life and that more abundant.

5) Working of Miracles

Miracles happen when there is no chance that something could have occurred in a usual or natural way. Mostly we see them in supernatural healings, such as new limbs growing out or organs reappearing that had been removed by surgery, or were never there when the child was born. I have heard of instances when a person was able to see and had no eyes to see with. Miracles are unexplainable, other than through the supernatural intervention of the Almighty God.

Though they are mostly related to health and healing of the body, they are by no means limited to it.

6) Prophecy

In the Old and the New Testaments we deal with prophecy. A Prophet is one through whom God speaks. He continues to speak to and through His people even in this New Covenant. I Corinthians 14:3 tells us about New Testament prophecy. *"But he that prophesieth speaketh unto men, edification, and exhortation, and comfort.* As I have previously explained, it did not pass away, but is needed to build up and strengthen the Church.

In Isaiah 58:1 we read, *"Cry aloud, spare not, lift up thy voice like a trumpet,..."*. the trumpet here symbolizes the prophetic voice.

There were two kinds of trumpets used in Israel. Some were made of ram's horns, the others were made of silver. The ram's horn trumpets represent natural Israel, or the Old Covenant. The silver trumpets represent the prophetic voice of the New Covenant, since silver is symbolic for redemption. We know that the celebrations of the Old Covenant Feasts, were a type and shadow of the New Covenant reality. The fact that there were rams horn and silver trumpets as well, shows the fact, that THERE WOULD ALSO BE NEW COVENANT PROPHETS.

There are also some in the New Covenant who are not Prophets, but at times will be able to give a prophetic word as the Spirit of God gives them a word to speak. This is as well found in the Old Covenant. An example of this is found in 1 Samuel 10:6-11, which talks about when King Saul met a group of Prophets and the Spirit of the Lord came UPON him for this specific purpose and he prophesied with them. Today, in the New Covenant Church one would probably say, that he or she felt an anointing to prophesy.

Revelation 19:10 says, *"..thy brethren that have the testimony of Jesus; worship God: for the testimony of Jesus is the Spirit of Prophecy."*

As I have already said about the gift of the word of Knowledge, the Prophet is not a psychic either. He or she can only speak the word which God has given to speak. If anyone thinks that by looking into a crystal ball one could know and speak about the future, that Prophet is not of God.

7) Discerning of spirits

This is definitely an important tool for godly living. It stops us from being deceived, since we would be able to see through the theatrics of the enemy. For instance: At times I may be speaking to someone and they are saying one thing, but the Holy Spirit will reveal to me their true motive. Sometimes I will even hear within myself the name of the spirit who is trying to deceive me. This gift is a most important tool to avoid falling into traps the enemy has set for us.

8) Diverse Kinds of Tongues

9) Interpretation of Tongues
I have explained these throughout this teaching.

CONCERNING ALL THE GIFTS OF THE SPIRIT, LET US REMEMBER THIS, THEY ARE GIVEN TO THE CHURCH (1Corinthians12:4-11), to build up and strengthen the Body of Christ. The gifts a person operates in are not just for this person. The gifts are for others. The only spiritual gift that is given when only the speaker is blessed and strengthened is tongues, the prayer language (1 Corinthians 14:3-4).

In 1 Corinthians 1:4-8, Paul writes,
"I thank my God always on your behalf, for the grace of God which is given you by Jesus Christ. That in every thing ye are enriched by Him, in all utterance, and in all knowledge; Even as the testimony of Christ was confirmed in you: So that ye come behind in no gift; waiting for the coming of our Lord Jesus Christ: Who shall also confirm you unto the end, that ye may be blameless in the day of our Lord Jesus Christ." **The word here used for gift is the Greek word "charisma" which is in the plural form "charismata" and speaks of gifts of a spiritual nature and divine endowment. Read this Scripture again and meditate on it.**
We need all the gifts, so that we can be strong and blameless when Jesus comes. Verse 7 and 8 both state that that these spiritual gifts will be with us and confirm and strengthen us unto the end, the day of our Lord Jesus Christ.
The fact that he uses the term *"even as"* in verse 6, shows that he is comparing the "charisma", or spiritual gift to something else. It is clear that he speaks of two

different things, the Gospel of Christ, and the other the gifts of the Spirit.

Often when speaking about the things of the Holy Spirit the word "anointing" is used. Though the word is frequently used through the entire Bible many still don't know it's meaning.

In the Old Testament individuals were set aside and marked for God with the anointing. A blend of very fragrant oils were mixed according to the LORD'S instructions.

What then is the anointing? The anointing is the enabling and empowering by the Spirit of God to perform a specific task in His Kingdom. It provides a special touch from God to accomplish what we have been sent forth to do.

Today believers often say that they could feel the anointing, which means that they felt the presence and touch of the Holy Spirit in a meeting or in their prayer time.

Often people say that their Pastor or worship leader was so anointed. This simply means that one could feel the Holy Spirit as they ministered.

In the New Testament Jesus and His disciples also anointed with oil and the people were set free. Mark 6:12-13 gives this account. *"And they went out, and preached that men should repent. And they cast out many devils, and anointed with oil many that were sick, and healed them."*

In James 5:14-15 we see the disciples continued anointing people, after Jesus ascended. *"Is any sick among You? Let him call for the elders of the Church; and let them pray over him, anointing him with oil and the prayer of faith shall save the sick, and the Lord shall raise him up; and if he have committed sins, they shall be for-given him."*

It remains a practice in the Church to this day and believers are still being helped by it.

I would briefly like to mention the MOTIVATIONAL GIFTS. Motivational gifts are not just spiritual gifts, but are actually a part of our personality makeup. They are called motivational gifts because they are what will set the person in motion, meaning, they are a motivating factor in that persons life to do what they think needs to be done. They are: mercy, giving, leadership, exhortation, teaching, serving and prophecy. Please read Romans 12:3-8.

People are created by the Father with these gifts. They are not the same as the gifts of the Holy Spirit, which are supernaturally imparted.

Even though prophecy is mentioned in the motivational gifts, it is not the same as prophecy, the gift of the Spirit. The motivational gift is rather an inborn sensitivity to the things of the Spirit and an ability to hear and speak what God brings to mind. It will often not even be recognized as being prophetic by the person who speaks it.

The Prophet in contrast to this knows when God is speaking. He or she, before the word is passed on to the people, often lets the listener know that it is God Who is doing the speaking.

12. WHAT A DIFFERENCE HE MAKES

R omans 14:19 instructs us, *"Let us therefore follow after the things which make for peace, and things wherewith one may edify another."* 1 Corinthians 14:1 tells us, *"Follow after charity and desire spiritual gifts, but rather that ye may prophesy."*

There should be a desire in every believers heart to operate in the gifts of the Spirit, not just for selfish exhibition, but for the strengthening of the Body of Christ, the Church. Paul shows partiality to prophecy, since it is such an important way to strengthen the believers.

In 1 Corinthians 14:3 he states that prophecy will edify, exhort and comfort. In other words, it will strengthen you, lift you up when you are down and comfort you when you are hurting. Paul wanted everything that God made available to us and truly pursued after it.

He knew that he didn't know it all and that he did not have it all yet. He says in Philippians 3:12, *"Not as though I had already attained, either were already perfect: but I follow after if that I may apprehend that for which also I am apprehended of Jesus Christ."*

If Paul admits that he does not know it all and is not perfect, and therefore desires more of God, how much more do we need the Holy Spirit and the gifts He brings.

There is a hunger among God's people to want more of Him. From my personal experience I can honestly say that I did not know what I was missing before I got baptized with the Holy Spirit. I thought that all that I already knew about God was all I needed to know. I could not imagine that with all the love I already felt from God, and all the blessing He had already given me, that there was more.

Having been a member of a major denomination I always thought that I was not lacking anything.

Since I had been leading worship for many years, I was visible in the Church. There was a gentleman who came to me frequently after service. He said that he could tell that I was a charismatic, and that they needed a worship leader in their charismatic meeting on Tuesday nights.

I did not even know what it meant to be charismatic. After at least a year of this man approaching me, I finally gave in and went to this meeting with my guitar.

As I walked into the Church for the first time, there was such great peace. There was such a sweet Spirit filling the sanctuary. I immediately realized that there was something I wanted but could not have known what that something was.

As I began to play and sing the love songs to the Lord, the people in the congregation began to sing in this beautiful language that I had never heard before. The prescence of the Spirit of God was tangeable. I had never felt anything like this in my life. When I experienced this awesome prescence of the Almighty God, I knew that I was in the right place.

The third Tuesday I was leading the worship in this meeting, an elderly woman was singing with me. Her hands were up in the air and her eyes were closed, when suddenly she began to sing in this heavenly language loud and clear.

As I looked at her something rose up in me. I opened my mouth and began to sing fluently in this marvelous language which I had never heard. It has to be said that no one laid hands on me. It came directly from the Holy Spirit.

From that day on there was a difference in my life. At the next meeting I noticed that I was able to see in the Spirit what was going on in the lives of the people in that congregation. I was able to recognize some of the infirmities with which they were battling. At times I saw the name of the disease written out in my mind. I was then able to call out these illnesses and some people were healed.

Shortly after this, in one of the meetings I had a strange heat in the area of my heart. My heart then began to beat fast and strong. As this marvelous heat increased in my physical heart there was an urging to speak out the words that I was hearing inside of me. When I then spoke these words out and gave them to the congregation, I felt a release in my heart. The prophetic had been released into my life. Since that day I grew in God and there is not always such a strong manifestation when I receive a Word from the Lord. I know the voice of God better now and when I recognize His voice, I just speak it out.

My life has totally changed since God filled me with the Holy Spirit. I was without it for many years and did not even know that there was more. Now, that I am baptized with the Holy Spirit I operate in different gifts of the Spirit, some to a greater, some in a lesser degree.

The Word of God began to open up for me. I understood the Word as I never understood it before. God began to instruct me in the night season in my dreams, and at times I have visions. My natural gift of music was easy for me to follow. Now, however, I teach and preach the Word of God. Since English is not my native tongue and I have never officially learned it, this is a miracle in itself.

The prophetic gift saved my life in 2005 before hurricane Katrina hit South Louisiana. In the beginning of that year I began to have dreams. In these dreams I was driving into St. Bernard Parish from East New Orleans. As I arrived at the main intersection in the town of Chalmette, I found everything destroyed by water. What I saw was so horrifying, that I was not even able to verbalize it. I had this dream three times, about every two months. Each time it was as if I had been kicked in my stomach.

About three weeks before the storm I had the last one. This time it had two parts to it. The first one again was the destruction of the Parish of St. Bernard, in the second I saw the disappearance of the entire West Bank of New Orleans. I saw that the Gulf of Mexico had come all the way to St. Bernard Highway in Chalmette. I felt so terrible to see this.

I was finally able to mention what I saw to a Bible study group about two weeks before Katrina.

As history can testify, it happened. It happened just as I saw it. The second part of the dream is still to be fulfilled concerning what I saw about the West Bank of New Orleans. I warn as many people as I can about this. Hopefully they will take it seriously.

I give You my testimony to let You know that I know these things are real, because I am experiencing them in my own life. I know the Baptism of the Holy Spirit is real and it is for You, if You have been born again. I have been without it, but now I have it and it made a big difference in my life.

Knowing and having this power in my life, I WANT TO PASS IT ON.

Some years ago I had a dream which was also prophetic. In it I was invited to minister in a Church. I remember the altar of that Church and the face of the man who was supposed to be the Pastor. Then I saw this person coming towards me. He had evil intentions, as I could see by what he was holding in his hands. I began to speak in tongues, rebuking him. This tongue came out in Spanish. Though I know only a few words in Spanish, I knew, that this was it. With the intensity only the Holy Spirit can put in a person, pointing my finger at him, I looked him straight in the eyes and spoke words that came almost like fire out of my mouth. As I awoke the Spirit of God told me what this man did. He had done a terrible thing to another person, and God even gave me the first name of the person he did it to.

I remembered many words I spoke in that dream and so called my Spanish speaking friend from Puerto Rico the next morning for interpretation. Indeed, they were real Spanish words and were within the context of this dream.

This is another proof that the gifts of the Spirit are real and are operating in the lives of God's people.

This dream has not come to pass yet. I will know this person definitely, who is pretending to be a man of God when I see him. I believe that God gave me a warning.

Once I was sharing God's love while shopping in a large home improvement store, when I met a young couple. They were new Christians. I prayed with them and God began to reveal to me some things going on in their lives. He even showed me things about their dog. The couple had never experienced the gifts of the Holy Spirit in operation and here were touched by the word of knowledge and prophecy. They were amazed and shared the experience with their Pastor.

About three months later, a member of the Church where the couple attended contacted me and within a few minutes connected me with the Pastor on a three way line.

The Pastor invited me to come to their next leadership meeting. I went. During the meeting the leaders were talking among themselves and asking whether their Church was ready for "what I had." I knew that God wanted to do something in this Church. While they were deciding about if they should vote to let me minister, the Pastor called me up. He asked me if I wanted to say something to the leadership group. I got up. Facing them these words just came out of my mouth. "It is the time for the visitation of the Lord, don't miss your visitation". About five minutes later they voted me in.

The Pastor, himself was an "unbeliever" in the Baptism of the Holy Spirit, speaking in tongues and the gifts of the Spirit. Strangely enough I was invited to the next Church service. I was given full freedom to move in the gifts as the Holy Spirit lead me. I gave a teaching for about 45 Minutes on the Baptism of the Holy Spirit and then began to minister to the people at the altar.

The entire congregation came to the altar, received the Holy Spirit and spoke in tongues that night, except the Pastor and his wife. One young man spoke in tongues and prophesied. The People were being delivered and set free. There was such a fire and presence of the Holy Spirit at the altar that the Pastor began to shout. It was undeniable.

There was an awesome move of God that night. Here was the Pastor of a traditional, large, major denominational Church, who himself did not believe; but God baptized everyone in his congregation that night with the Holy Spirit right before his eyes. He later could not make any other statement except, "I saw it, I saw it."

13. HOW CAN I RECEIVE THIS BAPTISM WITH THE HOLY SPIRIT

O ne way is by the laying on of hands of someone who has it. In Acts 19:6 we read, *"And when Paul laid his hands upon them, the Holy Ghost came upon them and they spake with tongues and prophesied."*

On another occasion Peter and John had gone to Samaria because they heard that there were believers. They had already been baptized into Christ but did not receive the Holy Spirit yet, the Promise of the Father. It is written in Acts 14:17, *"Then laid they* (Peter and John) *their hands on them, and they received the Holy Ghost."*

At another time the Holy Spirit just fell upon all of those who heard the Word. Acts 10:44-46 says, *"While Peter yet spake these words, the Holy Ghost fell on all them which heard the Word. And they of the circumcision which believed were astonished, as many as came with Peter, because that on the Gentiles also was poured out the gift of the Holy Ghost. For they heard them speak with tongues and magnify God...."*

Notice that they ALL spoke in tongues when the Holy Spirit came upon them.

I have come across many people in my ministry who have a fear of the Baptism of the Holy Spirit, simply because they don't understand it or have been taught that it is not for now. Some were even taught that speaking in tongues, prophecy, and other things associated with it are of the devil. To ascribe something to the devil which is of God, or even speak against the Holy Spirit is blasphemy which shall not be forgiven. To let you be at peace I have to add to this, that if you love God and want to be forgiven, you have not done this. The Holy Spirit is with you. I need to give you this Scripture however, Matthew 12:31, *"...all manner of sin and blasphemy shall be forgiven unto men; but the blasphemy against the Holy Ghost shall not be forgiven unto men."*

If you want to be baptized with the Holy Spirit, ask God for it. In Luke 11:9-13 Jesus says, *"And I say unto you, Ask, and it shall be given you; seek, and ye shall find; knock, and it shall be opened unto you. For every one that asketh receiveth; and he that seeketh findeth; and to him that knocked it shall be opened. If a son shall ask bread of any of you that is a father, will he give him a stone? Or if he asks for a fish, will he for a fish give him a serpent? Or if he shall ask an egg, will he offer him a scorpion? If ye then being evil, know how to give good gifts unto your children: how much more shall your Heavenly Father give the Holy Spirit to them that ask Him?*

We see here in the words of Jesus that a human father would be good to his children, therefore God, our Heavenly Father would freely give the Holy Spirit to those who ask and are already His children. This statement also reveals that Salvation is a separate experience from the Baptism of the Holy Spirit. First one has to become a child of God through faith in Christ, before the gift of the Holy Spirit will be given. Everyone who asks receives.

In order to receive the Baptism with the Holy Spirit the believer has to completely trust God. The Word tells us that we are not to lean on our own understanding. It also tells us that our human understanding remains unfruitful, meaning, we do not know what we are saying. Praying in tongues requires a total surrender, an abandonment of self to the Holy Spirit. According to the Apostle Paul praying in tongues is praying in the Spirit.

At times people rationalize, are fearful or unbelieving, and therefore have a problem yielding themselves to the Holy Spirit. Other hindrances could be that the individuals still have unconfessed and unrepentant sin in their lives. One must also understand that the Holy Spirit will not just take over the individuals vocal cords, tongue or lips. The Word tells us that *"And they were all filled with the Holy Ghost and began to speak in tongues as the Spirit gave them utterance."* (Acts 2:4) This means that He, the Holy Spirit, gave them what to say, but THEY HAD TO DO THE SPEAKING. At times it will only be one or two syllables, just like a child which has begun to talk. Others immediately have a fluent language.

In my many years of ministering, I personally am aware of only two people who began to sing in the Spirit rather than speak when they got baptized in the Holy Spirit. One is an elderly catholic lady, the other one is myself. I am sure that there are many more, but it is according to my experiences unusual.

I believe that the Holy Spirit, already living in the believer, will rise up when the person yields him or her self to be baptized with the Holy Spirit. Gifts that have laid dormant will suddenly come to life and new gifts will be given.

Occasionally there are people who have a little problem yielding themselves and giving up control to the Holy Spirit. These are the ones who rationalize everything or those who are afraid because they had been taught against it. They are the exception rather than the rule and are truly only a few. When they are able to yield, they will receive.

Remember to yield your voice to the Lord, and He will give you the expression.

The important thing that I want the reader to understand is that this precious gift of the Holy Spirit is according to Ephesians 1:14 the *"earnest"*, or down payment of our inheritance.

In the words of Paul to the Philippians 3:12, *"Not as though I had already attained, either were already perfect: but I follow after, if that I may apprehend that for which also I am apprehended of Christ Jesus."*

Get a hold of what Christ has made available to you. Go after it. He paid an awesome price. Don't let anything be in vain.

Do you want everything that God has for you? Walk in love and increase in it. Ask your Heavenly Father for spiritual gifts, so that you can be a blessing to those who need encouragement, healing and deliverance.

There is always more to God than our human minds can comprehend. There are always higher levels we can reach in God if we humbly acknowledge that we don't know it all.

PRESS IN !!!

In the words of Jesus in John14:26, *"But the Comforter, which is the Holy Ghost, Whom the Father will send in My Name, He shall teach you all things, and bring all things to your remembranc, whatsoever I have said unto you."*

It is also my prayer and desire for those who read this teaching "Sealed with the Spirit," that the Holy Spirit will bring to your remembrance all things that I have said.

If You are not sure that You are a child of God and if Your sins have been forgiven say this prayer.

In the Book of Romans 10:9-10 it tells us that with the heart we believe, but with the mouth we accept our Salvation.

Lord Jesus, I believe that You are the Son of God, that You died for my sins on the cross and You rose from the dead. Wash me clean in Your Precious Blood and come into my heart. I accept You as my Lord and Savior. Thank You Jesus for taking my place on the cross. Thank You for saving me.

14. SUMMARY

T he Baptism of the Holy Spirit did not pass away with the early Church. It was given to the CHURCH to help us in our battles.

That which is perfect has not yet come. We are told in Ephesians 1:14, that the Holy Spirit is a form of down payment on our heavenly inheritance, until Jesus comes to claim His purchased possession.

There are different kinds of tongues. One is the prayer language which is men speaking to God, the other is a prophetic tongue, God speaking to men. (Isaiah 28:11) It must be interpreted, since God is speaking to men.

The prayer language is for everyone. It is the initial sign of the Holy Spirit Baptism. It does not have to be interpreted, since it is directed towards God.

When we accept Christ, the Holy Spirit lives inside of us. When one is baptized with the Holy Spirit, the Holy Spirit comes upon the believer, fills them from above and seals them. The believer receives power when the Holy Spirit comes upon them.

There are nine gifts of the Spirit. Each gift is still for our time, until we have been perfected and things have been made right here on earth. They are needed for battle. The Holy Spirit will teach us and remind us of what we have learned.

The prophetic gift is to edify the Church. Tongues, the prayer language is a direct communication with God, bypassing the understanding. It will also strengthen and edify the speaker.

THE BAPTISM WITH THE HOLY SPIRIT IS FOR YOU. GO AFTER IT.
   BE FILLED WITH THE SPIRIT!!!!!

CPSIA information can be obtained
at www.ICGtesting.com
Printed in the USA
LVHW032302270520
656772LV00002B/714